A FIREMAN'S LIFT

*The funnier side
of a Firefighter's life*

Malcolm Castle

Illustrations
by
Woot

GET Publishing

First published in Great Britain in 2007
by GET Publishing, Bridgnorth, Shropshire WV15 5DG
info@getpublishing.co.uk

Copyright © 2007 Text Malcolm Castle
Copyright © 2007 Illustrations Chris Wootton
ISBN 978-0-9556464-5-4

Printed in the United Kingdom by
Hobbs Ltd, Brunel Road, Totton, Hampshire, SO40 3WX

CONTENTS

For Karen,
For life.

FOREWORD

If we've been asked once, we've been asked a thousand times, "So what is it you really do as a Firefighter?" A nickname we are often sunk with is 'Watersquirters'. This is because some people assume that all we do is simply pour thousands of gallons of water on a fire and flood it out. To be fair, this technique has great appeal sometimes, especially when you are the one who's actually got to enter the burning building. But alas no, not only do we have to put most fires out from the inside, but actual property fires make up only a small part of a Firefighter's job. We also find ourselves being called out to car accidents, chemical spills, or cats up chimneys, along with the more unusual jobs such as a pregnant cow stuck in a slurry pit or an unfortunate parachutist stranded in the top of a tree. The fact is, that if you have a problem and the Police, Ambulance, Coastguard, or even Breakdown service can't help you, all you are left with is the good old Fire Service. Now we don't actually mind this, for as the saying goes, 'Variety is the spice of life,' and there is an enormous amount of satisfaction to be gained from being presented with a problem you've never had before and sorting out a solution.

The success of the modern Fire Service owes a lot to our equipment, which is regularly updated and is, for the most part, at the forefront of technology. The problem we constantly face, however, is that in order to have the right tool for all possible scenarios, we would have to have a fleet of fire engines in attendance at every incident. Even then I'm sure there's bound to be a situation where we would be found lacking. So what's the answer? The answer is adaptability and ingenuity helped along by a generous portion of common sense. With the help of these we are able, in most cases, to live up to the high standard that the general public quite rightly demand.

You can imagine, I'm sure, that with the thousands of 'shouts' we turn out to there are bound to be occasional situations where plan A does not work quite so well in practice as it did in theory, and plan B needs to be put into action. This is, of course, just as soon as someone can come up with it. There is also the situation where the scenario is so obscure that any normal procedure is out of the question, and the 'make it up as you go along' drill is put into action.

Within this infinitely varied job of ours, there are obviously many humorous things that happen, some of which, for litigation reasons, cannot be published; but of those which can, I have attempted to choose the best to share with you.

I hope you enjoy them.

THE TALE OF THE SOGGY MOGGY

"Spag Bol ready on the hatch," came booming over the tannoy system. It was half past nine in the evening and tonight Dale had made his famous spaghetti bolognese. We were all famished, so hearing his message started the familiar stampede to the mess room to get there first so as to decide which was the biggest portion and casually choose that one. One by one the steaming meals were taken to the table where the garlic bread, parmesan cheese, and various other relishes awaited the hungry firemen.

Now Sod's Law is a strange old thing which many will argue doesn't exist, but... you sit down to an eagerly-awaited meal and you can bet your bottom dollar that if you were going to have a call-out that night, then that's when you would get it!

So here it was. The tannoy boomed again... "Water Tender Ladder to an animal rescue at Whichurch." With a collective groan all of us got up and made our way as quickly as we could to the appliance room on the ground floor. Only one fire engine had been called for, but it is standard practice for us all to go downstairs in case someone trips and injures themselves on the way down and needs to be replaced on the fire engine. No one was injured today so five of us got on board and were dispatched with a

pseudo-sympathetic wave by those left to finish their meal. Obviously they received various other gestures in return!

Whichurch was a twenty minute drive away, and on the way we learned that the animal in need of rescuing was, in fact, a cat. It belonged to a lady who was utterly distraught because her dear little furry friend was stuck up the chimney. Earlier that evening it had been startled by a car backfiring outside and dashed for cover.

We eventually arrived at Cornelia Close and knocked on the door of number 27. We waited a short while before knocking again, a little louder this time. "I'm coming," came a little voice from inside. After what seemed like an age the door opened. There stood a tiny old lady, smartly dressed with her grey hair pulled back tightly into a neat bun. "I'm so glad you're here, come on in, gosh aren't you all big, 'scuse the mess, go on through, she's in there," she said without taking a breath. So in we went, four big burly firemen squeezing past dear little Flora (as she introduced herself) and into the living room. There in front of us was the chimney up which the cat, named Newby, was stuck. Leading Firefighter Gordon Bains, our officer in charge, said in his usual droll manner, "Well lads, no good just looking at it, clear the decks, and let the dog see the rabbit." So we 'cleared the decks,' moving the coal bucket, the fire irons, the log box, the various horse brasses, and the quaint little porcelain cat which sat with a rather snooty expression in the corner of the hearth. This done, we gathered round the fire and listened, and looked, and listened some more.

Nothing could be seen or heard of poor Newby and we began to discuss the possibility that she might have got herself out. Suddenly, Gordon hissed, "Quiet lads did you hear something?" We stopped and listened …. nothing. But Gordon insisted he had heard a faint meow and this was all we needed to convince ourselves that Newby was, indeed, still trapped up the chimney and it was up to us to rescue her.

Well, we tried everything: shining torches up from the bottom, then climbing up onto the roof and shining torches down from above. We tried tempting the unhelpful feline down with her favourite food, and getting Flora to kneel close to the fire place and call up the chimney, "Come down my sweet, come to mummy." All this came to nothing. Newby, we decided was a stubborn blinkin' creature and a more drastic approach was required. It was decided to take a hosereel from the fire engine up onto the roof and dribble a little water down to persuade the cat to get out from whichever nook or cranny it was hiding in. We were in contact with the guys on the roof by radio and the order was given to squirt a momentary burst of water down the chimney. This was done, but no cat appeared. Another slightly longer burst was asked for. Again no cat. A third burst fuelled with frustration saw black water starting to stream down into the fireplace. But still no damn cat.

So there we were. Plans A, B, C, and D had been thought up and professionally executed but still the poor, dirty, and by now probably sodden, little Newby was not

rescued. We might have been tempted to give up but her pitiful meows could occasionally be heard and Flora was becoming increasingly anxious.

We had been at this job for over an hour and the various messages sent back had aroused the interest of Brian Reeves, an officer driving locally in his car whilst monitoring the fire service radio. He decided to add his tu'penny ha'pennys worth to the rescue so drove to the address and came striding into the house, tall, arrogant, and generally dislikeable. "What's up gents, not got it down yet then?" There was a general biting of lips as Gordon explained the situation in words of one and two syllables. Now officers of this type like to make big decisions. They have the power and by God they're going to weald it. So, after being fully briefed as to where we were, Reeves stood up to his full height and smugly declared, "Well surely it's obvious! There is a shelf in the chimney about four feet up, cut a hole in the chimney breast and fetch the cat out that way."

Well, far be it for us to disregard the advice of an officer, so after okaying it with dear old Flora we started knocking bricks out of the chimney breast at the same height as the ledge inside the flue. Dust burst into the room with every strike of the chisel and began settling on all the lace cushions and neatly arranged photographs on the antique sideboard. We would of course clean up the mess before we left, but we hadn't finished making it yet. Reeves had heard the cat himself and was eagerly awaiting the conclusion of the job brought on by his brave and dynamic decision. It was

down to me to put my arm into the hole to retrieve the stricken creature, but, after a tentative feel around, nothing was to be found. Reeves couldn't believe it and demanded to do the job properly himself.

Just then a strange coincidence occurred… Flora offered a cup of tea and left to the kitchen to make it, and little Newby gave her loudest meow yet. A certain paleness came over Reeve's face because, much to our surprise, the meow hadn't come from where his hand was now buried. It came from just to one side of the chimney - the log box to be precise. Smug comments had to be stifled when we opened up the box to reveal the trapped Newby.

Unfortunately Flora chose just that moment to come back in to find out who wanted sugar. She started asking while she was still out in the kitchen. "Quick, give me that cat!" barked Reeves. Quick as a flash he stuffed the poor creature into the hole and jiggled it round the inside of the dirty and wet chimney. Just as Flora came through the door, he pulled the now black and soggy moggy out of the hole and said with an overly sympathetic flourish, "Look Flora we've rescued Newby. She's safe and sound now, all is well."

Flora was delighted, we were heroes, Reeves was unbearable, and the cat? Well, she could consider herself well and truly rescued.

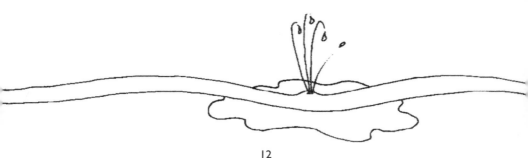

WHO NEEDS ENEMIES

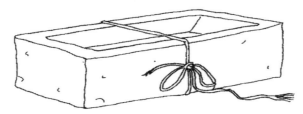

Farms, as I'm sure most farmers would agree, can be dangerous places. Heavy machinery with sharp blades, slurry pits, farm buildings with loopholes and trapdoors in the floor are just some of the dangers which all too often cause injury to farmers and their employees. The risk of serious injury is therefore much greater to unsuspecting townsfolk who don't see the hidden dangers.....

It was a warm summer Sunday afternoon when we received a call to proceed to "A PERSON TRAPPED UNDER LARGE STRAW BALES" at a farm just outside Shrewsbury. The Leading firefighter responded to the radio message and we were on our way, pleased to be doing a real job as opposed to the fire hydrant tests that had taken up the early part of our afternoon. On route it was agreed that if the 'large straw bales' that the control staff had mentioned had fallen on the casualty, we would probably be recovering a body, as each round bale weighs almost a ton. After a journey of some fifteen minutes and a great deal of nifty map reading, we arrived at the incident to be met by a young man directing us into the farm yard.

Running ahead, he led us to the barn and the scene of the incident. The bales were indeed the large round type, all stacked neatly like baked bean tins, one on top of the other, four bales high. The casualty had, for some reason, been on top of the stack and slipped down the hole created where four stacks of bales met. He had slid down to ground level, a drop of some twenty feet and his rather slurred answers to questions shouted down to him by the Lf led us to believe that he was either drunk or injured.

Various well-dressed people were stood about showing limited amounts of concern, happy to tell us that, "We've been talking to him, he's OK, he just can't get himself out." It was at about this time the farmer arrived demanding, as was his right, to know the meaning of this invasion, which by now amounted to two fire engines, an ambulance, a fire service officer and a policeman. It turned out that the casualty had been attending a sixtieth birthday party at a property across the road. Some of the children present were bored and our man had offered to accompany them on an adventure to the farmyard. We never did find out exactly why he had climbed to the top of the stack but fortunately for him, after his mishap, the children had the good sense to return to the party and raise the alarm.

We put it to the farmer that the bales would have to be removed and, although reluctant, he agreed that we had no choice. The top bales were removed by simply pushing them down but things were done a little more carefully as we got nearer the bottom. On removing the last bale we were shocked to find our casualty slumping, his head covered with dark sticky blood some of which had dried

on his face and clothing leaving him looking more like the victim of a road traffic accident than a man who'd slipped down between some straw bales.

We called the ambulance crew in and our part of the rescue was complete. All that remained for us was to make our equipment up whilst our Lf collected details for the special service report form. We mounted the truck, ready to leave the incident but were still waiting for the Lf who was deep in conversation with one of the ambulance crew. A peep on the horn hurried him along, his grin getting bigger as he approached the truck and climbed aboard. "No," he said holding back a giggle, "it's not funny, we shouldn't laugh. C'mon lets go." We took off, eager to hear the full story as told to him by the ambulance attendant....

The kids, as we already knew, had rushed back to the party alerting various adults as to the accident. Several ran across to the barn and quickly made contact with the entrapped but uninjured man. Realising that they were trespassing and with a good measure of alcohol inside each, they decided the best move was to release him themselves. Their plan was to lower a length of rope for the casualty (not knowing that his arms were pinned by his sides) who would simply grab hold and be pulled up to safety; they would surely be back at the party in no time, laughing about the whole incident. Unfortunately their plan ran into a problem almost immediately when no rope could be found. Not to worry, someone had found a couple of lengths of baler twine that, once tied together, would be just the ticket. The next problem was that, no matter how hard

they tried, the baler twine would not go down the hole as it kept catching on the straw that stuck out all around. What was needed was a small weight on the twine to aid its descent, something like ummm......... I know, a house brick.

A brick was found and duly tied to the twine; the rescue was under way. Well at least it was, until the twine suddenly became very light, and there was a sickening 'thud' followed by a muffled scream. The poor chap could hear it coming but couldn't even lift his arms to protect himself and, yes, the brick hit him square on the head after a drop of about ten feet, causing a serious laceration and severe concussion although thankfully not a fractured skull. This in itself was not really that funny, (oh all right, it was) but what had amused us most was the fact that amongst all the 'friends' standing round, not one person had the guts to come up and tell us, "oh yeh, we know he's down there cause we've just dropped a brick on his head."

With friends like that.................

FLUSHED WITH SUCCESS

Fire-calls at meal times are sometimes met by firefighters with groans of disapproval, especially at breakfast time when a gruelling 15-hour night shift is drawing to a close. So it was with little excitement the Emergency Tender (ET) crew turned out to a 'person trapped in a toilet.' This is a common call for the fire service which, more often than not, ends up with a firefighter up a ladder peering in through the opening light of the toilet window and using his best powers of persuasion to talk little Johnny into unlocking the door. Nine times out of ten the youngster, oblivious to all the fuss he has caused, will, after promises of a 'sit on the fire engine' or similar treats, unlock the door and be greeted by his relieved and grateful mother. If that tried and tested method fails it may be time to bring Fire Service initiative in to play, using various implements such as chimney rods or a pitchfork in an effort to reach the door lock whilst still on the ladder. If all else fails then the door must be forced and, although we endeavour to keep damage to a minimum, the poor child may be left to explain the reason for the cracked and splintered door to Daddy when he gets home from work.

This however was not to be the case that morning, and after a short trip to the given address the ET crew, a Leading firefighter (Lf) and one firefighter, were met by an anxious and tearful lady in her fifties who led the crew to the kitchen door. It was not a modern house and by the general state of the place the colleagues assumed that renovation work must be in progress. On entering the premises the pair were shocked to see a human leg wearing a tartan slipper with a furry pom-pom on the toe hanging lifelessly from the kitchen ceiling. Upon enquiry they were able to ascertain that the lady was the mother of the person at the other end of the leg, and had just popped in from her own house across the road to visit her daughter for morning coffee. On entering the house through the kitchen door she had encountered the same sight as the ET crew and after an initial failed attempt to free her unfortunate offspring she realised, to her daughter's horror, that the Fire Service must attend. A rescue plan was quickly put into action with the immediate priority being to provide a stepladder for the foot in question to rest upon. Whilst this task was being carried out, mother filled the lads in on the history of this most unusual incident.

The house was, as the lads suspected, in the process of being renovated, although a few 'dodgy' floorboards were still in place, some of these being in the upstairs WC. The toilet, according to Mother (the crew never did see it), was a relatively long and narrow room with the 'throne' being directly opposite the door, on which the loo roll hung. Her son-in-law had risen, breakfasted and left for work leaving his wife asleep in bed. A little later she rose, went downstairs for breakfast then returned upstairs to wash and dress after first visiting the 'little girls room'. From the size of the leg the lads were able to guess at the weight and build of the lady in question (and they were thinking big). They could well understand why, whilst sitting on the toilet and leaning forward, putting all her weight on her leading foot to reach for the paper, a rotten floorboard had given way. The poor girl could reach neither the toilet chain nor loo roll but instead was left sitting on the floor with one thigh horizontally out to her left with knee bent and the calf and foot twisted back behind her whilst the right leg was left dangling through the kitchen ceiling up to... well, as far as it could be.

In a modern house with chipboard floors and plasterboard ceilings the rescue would have been far less arduous but with traditional, if somewhat rotten, floorboards and a lath and plaster ceiling to deal with, a delicate touch would be required. The main problem for the unlucky colleagues was that when a leg (large or otherwise) is forced down through that type of ceiling, the lathes that hold the plaster in place split and bend downwards, but if you try to force the limb back up through the hole they close up again not unlike a set of jaws. This was also the case, to a lesser degree, with the floorboards above.

After a brief discussion the brave boys decided that the only way to free the casualty was to very carefully cut the laths and floorboards away using a hand saw and hacksaw blade, a delicate job indeed. The Lf nominated his colleague who positioned himself on the step ladder and began his unenviable task. As he was to explain later, "The more I cut away the more I could see." Eventually the cutting away was completed and with Mother helping upstairs the bruised and scratched leg was gently pushed back up from whence it came. After enquiring with Mother as to the young lady's condition and recommending professional medical attention the crew collected the necessary details, gathered their tools and left the scene without ever meeting the casualty, as this seemed in the circumstances the kindest thing to do.

It was for some time after the incident that when out on the fire engine we paid particular attention to the 'larger ladies' that we saw going about their daily business. "Ere she's limping a bit," or "she looked a bit embarrassed to see us, didn't she," were typical comments. The incident report would have told us her name and, of course, we already knew her address but I don't think the ET crew really wanted to meet her; they do say that first impressions are lasting impressions!

A TERMINAL PROBLEM

It was a gloriously hot bank holiday Monday. The fire station appliance room was buzzing with the noise of firefighters doing the morning checks. This involved making sure that all the equipment carried on the fire engines was where it should be and in working order. The breathing apparatus sets were also being checked to make sure that they were in perfect condition; you really don't want to go into a burning building without knowing that the thing that's keeping you alive is in tip top working order! In the real world, outside this hive of activity, families in their thousands were driving to beaches, wildlife parks, and all manner of other places promising a 'fun-filled' time, but in order to get there they must first experience the bank holiday nightmare .... the traffic jam.

It's always been an unfortunate fact that virtually all workers in Britain have the same bank holidays off. This means that they are forced to all go away for "a couple of days" at the same time. Of course the result is that the main holiday routes get filled with cars full of irate overheated parents, and sickly or annoying kids. It's no wonder then that bank holidays are notorious for what we refer to as Road Traffic Collisions. True to form, this particular Easter bank holiday produced an RTC caused by some impatient driver overtaking without enough room. His vain attempts to get back on his side of the road created a multiple 'pile up' involving six cars. A minute or so later the tannoy at the fire station interrupted our morning routines by turning out one fire engine and the emergency tender. This latter vehicle has specialised cutting and lifting equipment on it and goes to all RTCs. We jumped aboard and started our journey, all of us quietly preparing ourselves for what we might be faced with... well almost all of us. We had with us today, a shiny new member of the watch, a jockey, and he was anything but calm. This was his first car accident and he was desperate to show us all how keen and clever he was. All the way to the incident he was excitedly remarking on things he could see out of the fire engine window - things one would always see, but for some reason on this trip they were utterly fascinating and needed to be commented on at high volume.

There are a number of set tasks we are responsible for when we first arrive at an RTC: we pull a hosereel off to cover the vehicles in case they burst into flames, we set up a 'tool dump' with the main tools we might need, one firefighter will deal with the glass in the car, removing it if required, one will protect the fire engine by coning it off and making sure no one crashes into us, and so on. You can see that there's a lot to do in a short time; and this is before we actually start the rescue itself.

It was difficult for us to get to the crash due to the number of queuing vehicles being held up by the blocked road. Many were attempting to turn round thus making our progress even harder but when we got within a hundred yards of the RTC most of the cars were empty with their occupants having got out to get a better look. It's human nature that people will often work really hard to get a glimpse of a gory scene, but

when they succeed they immediately turn away with revulsion, only to turn back a little later for another look.

So, eventually, we pulled up at the incident. Everyone knew what needed doing and got on with doing it. That is, all except young Nicolas Beardsmore, the jockey, who simply ran around desperately looking for a task where he could show the rest of us just how good he was. After less than a minute of running backwards and forwards, our officer in charge noticed his dilemma and called him over to give him a job. "Now young Beardsmore, I want you to make all these vehicles safe, do you understand what that means?"

"Of course Sir, I'll get on with it right away," came back the excited reply, and off he ran. The term "make cars safe" simply refers to disconnecting the battery of the vehicle thus reducing the risk of creating an electrical spark. This is something you definitely don't want, what with all the spilled petrol fumes in the vicinity. We try to disconnect the terminals using a spanner if there might be some chance of repairing the vehicle, but more often than not we simply cut them because the vehicle is way beyond any chance of being fixed.

So, young Beardsmore decided that the quickest and most impressive method was the latter one and once armed with the appropriate cable cutters, proceeded to cut battery terminals with gusto. He was just finishing the fourth set when he was spotted by the officer in charge. "STOP!!! What do you think you're doing Beardsmore? You're only supposed to be doing the cars involved in the accident... not those in the queue!!"

JUMP....
you'll be down in no time

"Hello… is that the Guinness Book of Records? Could you tell me who holds the record for the longest parachute jump, because we think we've found someone to beat it."

This is what we should have done after returning from a particularly challenging incident one beautiful June day. It had started with the usual minimal information on the turnout sheet. All it said was, "person stuck in tree." The fact that the address was the local parachute club should have started alarm bells ringing, but it was such a hot day that the act of putting two and two together was simply too much like hard work.

We turned up at Montford Bridge Parachute Club to be greeted by someone who is apparently referred to as a "sky god". He was dressed in a well worn, over colourful and baggy jump suit, with long limp hair scraped back into a pony tail, and sporting an obligatory pair of open-toed sandals. "Hey guys, good to see you at last. I thought you'd got lost…can I cadge a lift? She's over there in the far corner; I'll show you." After resisting the knee jerk reply which was on all of our lips, we brought him into the fire engine and allowed him to state the blinkin' obvious in directing us down to the end of the one and only runway, which in fact we were already on.

Twenty minutes earlier a terrified Vanessa Sargent had been perched in the doorway of a small aeroplane 2800' above the airfield. When the order to jump was yelled in her ear she closed her eyes, said a little prayer and then jumped. She should have shouted, "One thousand … two thousand … three thousand… check canopy," but it's hard to do this when you're still praying, and your eyes are still shut. They remained shut for the majority of the descent to earth, only opening when the instructor's initially encouraging voice speaking through a megaphone, became a manic scream warning her that if she didn't do a bit of steering she was going to land in the.… too late! She disappeared into the middle of the only copse of trees for miles with the accuracy of a darts player scoring a bulls-eye.

So this was the scene we were now facing. Poor Vanessa was hanging in her harness yards from the nearest tree trunk with her parachute laid beautifully over the highest branches of the trees.

This was a small copse of trees; so small in fact that no one walked through it, they walked round. Thus it was completely overgrown with brambles, small saplings and various other plant life creating a barrier like the one surrounding Sleeping Beauty's castle.

Therefore, as in a scene from" Mission Impossible," our job, although we had no choice but to accept it, was to somehow get through the undergrowth and rescue the beautiful young lady before Julian, the 'sky god' could proffer

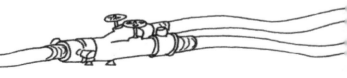

some other 'helpful' remark. Firstly we had to come up with a plan. The flippant suggestion of levitation was rejected and we decided to climb up to her using one of our long ladders. This, one would think, should have occurred to us earlier but, as I said, it was very overgrown in there and we didn't have anything to lean the ladder against (a pretty essential requirement, we find).

However…we fetched our longest ladder from off the roof of the fire engine and made our way to the copse. This ladder is 4m long when it is at its shortest and a metre wide, so you can imagine that threading it through the undergrowth without being able to bend it took several attempts. By the way, did I say it was a hot day?

When we eventually got the ladder to below Vanessa we were sweating cobs. You see, our "fair damsel in distress" was watching our every move so there was an added incentive to make the ladder appear light and manoeuvring it no effort at all to us strong, capable firefighters. So now, inwardly exhausted, we hatched a plan to reach our target. We first tied ropes to either side of the top of the ladder, then, with a firefighter on each rope, pulled it into an upright position. Next we extended it upwards to one side of Vanessa, then tied off the ropes to convenient tree trunks. Thus we had succeeded in getting the ladder into a working position without leaning it against anything. We felt justifiably proud of ourselves even though it had taken thirty-five minutes to get to this position and she still wasn't technically rescued yet.

Now came the biggest decision. Who was actually going up to rescue the delectable Vanessa? After a short, whispered, and yet heated discussion, rank was pulled and our officer in charge nominated himself for the task. With our disgruntled faces looking upwards we watched as Leading Firefighter, John Penlington, climbed the ladder. Having reached his goal he spent a surprisingly long time "consoling the casualty" before helping her onto the ladder and out of her harness. With all macho guns blazing he eased her down, one rung at a time, until she reached the ground. This meant that it had been exactly 57 minutes from when Vanessa had made her fateful exit from the plane, until she hit terra firma; which is why, as I said at the start, we should have contacted the Guiness Book Of Records upon our return.

"Don't go in the water"

There was no doubt in my mind - it just had to be the hottest day of the year so far. I found myself wondering where I would prefer to be. My options seemed clear enough; on a beach somewhere with a cool beer or here, on the drill ground wearing a thermal fire tunic and running round like a thing possessed. My ponderings were brought to a rather abrupt end by Station Officer Alan. He was bawling at me that as the 'new boy' on the watch I might perhaps show a little interest in the ladder and pump drill I was about to begin. We had to pretend that the third floor of the solid brick practice building was on fire, and we needed to enter at that level to rescue some imaginary fair damsel in distress. Luckily for me, in the next moment this often repeated and terminally boring scenario was to be replaced by something altogether more interesting.

The order, "Get to work!" had barely left Phillip Alan's lips when a call came over the tannoy: 'EMERGENCY TENDER AND WATER TENDER TO A COW IN THE RIVER AT MONTFORD BRIDGE'. I had only been going out on emergency calls for seven months and as I had been assigned to the water tender that day I let out an involuntary whoop of excitement at going to yet another one. There were other whoops, but they were from the older hands who had just been given an excuse to stop the drill.

It was approximately four miles to the bridge in question. Plenty of time to boost my youthful ego at all the faces looking at us driving through the town, lights flashing, horns blaring. I felt like a child on his favourite fairground ride with a grin from ear to ear and heart pumping like crazy. It's a strange thing but even now after twenty-six years in the service I still get a certain thrill whenever we turn out to an incident. I also can't help feeling the way Moses must have felt when we are confronted by a seemingly impenetrable mass of vehicles in front of us. Just by operating the two-tone horns the traffic parts, just like the Red Sea, leaving us just enough room to simply drive right through, and what a special feeling that is. Anyway back to the story. After a few minutes we arrived at the incident. We turned off the road and into a lush green pasture. The river formed the border on two sides and with the sun glinting off its surface it presented us with an idyllic summer scene. Over to the far right corner was the farmer waving at us to come to him. We obliged and were greeted by a ruddy- faced old man who shouted at us even before we were off the machine. "'Er's in 'ere mon," which roughly translated meant, 'She is in here mate.' We gathered round to see the cause of his concern and were faced with a cow, up to her shoulders in the river. It should be noted at this time that the poor thing appeared quite happy to be there and a look of complete indifference seemed to sweep over her face when confronted by the seven of us peering down at her.

After a short discussion, a command decision was made. Bob and Stick, two experienced hands, were to fetch a rope and make a lasso. This they did and in true Roy Rogers style attempted to throw the loop over the cow's neck. After a pitiful display all they had managed to do was drive the animal further out into the middle of the river. It was time for a rethink, and unfortunately for me (as it was to turn out) Plan B was not long in coming. Old Cassy, as he was affectionately known, stepped up and in his southern Shropshire droll uttered those words which even now strike a note of fear in my heart. "What we need 'ere is someone to go in after 'er. We're gonna be 'ere all day watchin' these two tryin' to lasso 'er. Now who's the tallest and newest one 'ere?" Unfortunately, at 6'4" I qualified on both counts. Thus, duly nominated, I was directed to strip, and go in after the cow. With no changing facilities to hand, and a small crowd of inquisitive onlookers gathering on the other bank, I attempted to maintain a little modesty by climbing into the rear cab of one of the fire engines to undress. After some interesting contortions I re-emerged sporting a pair of blue Y-fronts (fresh that morning thankfully) and did my best 'but I always wear these for swimming' walk towards the river bank. The obligatory barrage of encouraging comments ensued. I did try to rise above them but with little success, so, red-faced, I ventured down the bank and into the water. By this time the cow was about 50 yards downstream of me so with my best Olympic dive I headed off after her. Now I don't know if you are aware of the fact, but cows are pretty handy in water so upon seeing me thrashing the water to a foam in my attempts to reach her, she just turned and headed off in the opposite direction, leaving me for dead. Well I swam, and I swam, and after ten minutes had never

been closer than 12 feet from her. Each time I came close she would give me a look of complete impunity, and simply swim away, but never in the direction of the bank, as was my aim.

Meanwhile my colleagues, and an increasing number of curious onlookers, were starting to shout helpful advice from either bank: "Swim like this," said one, waving his arms in some unrecognisable stroke. "Swim underwater at 'er," said another. There were other less helpful suggestions offered, but as most of them referred to my possible sexual persuasions towards our ruminant friends, I'll spare you the details.

Eventually, I did manage to get the cow near enough to the bank for the by now hysterical firemen to put a loop of rope tied to a long branch, over her head. The poor thing put up quite a struggle at their attempts to 'rescue' her, but she was no match for six good firemen and true, and was unceremoniously hauled up the bank and into the field. The loop was then removed and without so much as a backward glance she trotted off to join her fellows grazing quite peacefully in the other corner of the pasture. As this was going on, I was dragging myself out of the water, looking and feeling like a damp squib. Unlike the cow, I couldn't have trotted anywhere, and barely made it to the refuge of the fire engine before collapsing in a wet heap to start the uncomfortable process of drip drying.

With the cow having been duly rescued, we re-stowed all our gear, and after being thanked by the farmer, headed off back to the fire station.

The following day, a bottle of whiskey was delivered to the fire station along with a note from the farmer. It read, 'Dear Red Watch, thank you for your help yesterday, you did a good job of rescuing the cow. Unfortunately, twenty minutes after you left, she was back in the river cooling off again but I decided not to call you out that time. It was O.K. though because she just walked out when she'd had enough.'

BEWARE OF
THE BOGEY MAN

You have to be very careful when you're on duty in the Fire Service. It doesn't matter where you are on station, or what you're doing, if you get a call out you have to drop everything and start running. It is actually your responsibility to get to the fire engine and out through the doors in under fifty seconds so there's no time for dawdling. Now of all the places you don't want to be caught in, the toilet has to be the worst, especially when you were expecting to be there for some time. In my years with the Fire Service I've only been caught in the toilet once. Unfortunately, the call out which caught me out was to a 'persons reported' (someone trapped in a burning building), so there was no time to complete the job in hand and do the necessary paperwork satisfactorily. Now the theory of stopping in mid flow is all fine and dandy, but actually doing it is quite another thing. It took a super human effort to halt nature's call and then, after a cursory clean up job, I was out through the door whilst still trying to haul my trousers up from around my knees.

The job which I found myself responding to was a fire in a terraced house. There were apparently two young boys trapped in the back bedroom so time was of the

essence. We normally drive quite quickly to any call-out, but where there is life at stake we always find that extra bit of speed which makes the journey feel all the more urgent. On the way there, two men were putting on their breathing apparatus sets and another was preparing to be responsible for them once they went into the job. The two B.A. men (as we call them) were Rob Jobson (a new watch member on his first persons reported), and Mark Chisel, an experienced hand.

We arrived at the address to be confronted by smoke billowing out of the rear of the house, and flames shooting high into the air. It was a spectacular sight, and one worth a good long looking at but we all had a far more pressing job to do. At an incident like this there is no time to waste, so everyone springs into action. The driver of the first fire engine makes sure there is water to use when needed. The two B.A. men start up their sets and pull the hosereel off the drum towards the fire. The man responsible for them takes their special identification tallies and records on them how much air they each have and when they should be coming out of the job. Other firemen will be making a quick search around the outside of the house to seek out helpful clues as to the whereabouts of any trapped people. Now, with all this activity going on it would be all too easy to simply barge into the house riding on a wave of adrenaline, but thankfully this rarely happens, and let me explain why...

Every fireman with any sense at all has a healthy respect about going into a burning building. All sensible people get out pretty damn quick, but with just a thick coat

and a breathing apparatus set to protect him, a firefighter is expected to go in, not only to rescue someone (which to be fair most people would attempt) but also to save a building.

Now there has to be a major flaw in your character if you get a kick out of saving a building which might have to be demolished afterwards anyway.

There are other reasons why going into a burning building is not a good idea. Like...

God in his wisdom gave us five senses, but we put on a full face mask and immediately lose smell and taste. In an average house fire the smoke is so thick you can't see your hand in front of your face even with a torch, that is even if you could see through the mask in the first place because it's normally covered with dirt and smut from the fire...so that removes sight. Fires are incredibly noisy, what with your own breathing, engines running outside, people shouting and so on, so hearing is of limited use. The only sense we are left with is touch, and the powers that be have (for our own protection) issued us with thermally insulated gloves, which make it almost impossible to distinguish between the arm of a sofa and casualty's thigh for example. Basically we are blind, and entering a building where we don't know if the floor will collapse underneath us or the ceiling will come down on top of us. We don't know if there is a calor gas cylinder in the next room just about to reach its explosive temperature and ready to go bang. We also don't know if a window is about to shatter and let in a rush of oxygen causing a backdraught, which has the same effect as a bomb going off. On top of that the temperature can be up to 900degrees celcius, hot enough to roast your Sunday joint four times over. Now it is in this 'chamber of horrors' that we have to try and find the trapped person. Hard enough you might think but, people do the strangest things in fires, like hiding from it under tables or behind wardrobes. So here you are, making your way through the house in the dark and the heat, knowing little about what might happen next when all of a sudden a body leaps on you from out of the darkness desperate to be rescued. The prospect of this happening is similar to a child's fear of the bogey man pouncing on them at night… irrational in the daylight but very real in the dark.

So, you can imagine that for our new watch member John Robson this was quite an overwhelming situation to be faced with. This is why inexperienced men are always sent in with experienced ones, and why, they stick pretty close to them once inside the building.

Mark took the lead and entered through the front door. Extinguishing any fire as they came across it, they made their way up the stairs to the bedroom at the rear of the house. In a room of this size we normally search it by splitting up. One searches left, one right, then after meeting in the far corner we come back diagonally across the middle of the room and then we deem it searched. On this occasion Mark went left and John went right. Almost immediately he came across the bed and in searching it found one of the boys still under the covers. He shouted

to Mark that he'd found one and was told to take him out while the second one was searched for. So with his heart in his mouth John carefully wrapped the boy in the quilt and carried him downstairs and out into the fresh air. "First Aid! First Aid!!!" he shouted as he emerged out of the house. There was a delay before one of the firefighters outside burst into laughter closely followed by everyone else within sight of the all-conquering hero standing before them. Shocked at their lack of concern, John wiped his dirty face mask and looked down at his rescued casualty. It was only then that he realised what all the laughter was about. Instead of cradling a small child in his arms he was dismayed to discover that in fact he was carrying, wrapped in a quilt, a three foot teddy bear!

The two boys had been discovered in the back garden of their friend's house next door, watching the spectacular sight of their house on fire; totally oblivious to the panic and commotion going on at the front. It was a pity that young John hadn't been made aware of this quite important detail prior to going in.

THE LIFT BUSTERS

Nowadays each emergency service has its own role to play at any given incident. However there are times when we must pull together for the common good in an effort to help each other out.

This 'helping each other out' was taken quite literally one cold morning in Telford about sixteen years ago. The watch were resting upstairs after a hectic night when, at about 5a.m., the front door bell rang and, after making himself look presentable at this early hour, the Sub Officer opened up to find a young police constable standing there. He was invited in but declined the offer, obviously keen to get straight down to business. He had been sent, it seemed, to request our help and expertise in a lift rescue at a nearby block of high rise flats. Such rescues are categorised under two headings: one being the rescue of persons trapped inside a lift car (usually fairly quick and painless) and the other, persons trapped in the workings of a lift, (much less common but it can be messy when it happens). Fortunately this was to be the former which, although better for all concerned, did not make the prospect of turning out yet again any more attractive. "No lights or horns," was the request from the police constable which of course referred to blue flashing lights and two-tone horns. Something was

not quite the ticket here and we all knew it. Firstly why send round the young copper when we regularly received calls from the police via our control? Secondly, although we don't use horns at that time of day if we can avoid it, why no flashing lights? Very odd!

On arrival we were met by a WPC who, poor girl, was suffering from a fit of the giggles which she desperately tried to suppress. At little more than a whisper she explained to the somewhat puzzled Sub Officer that there were indeed people stuck in the lift car, between the fifth and sixth floors, and the reason for the low key approach was that they were all members of the Drug Squad who were, until this unfortunate mechanical hiccup, engaged on a 'bust'. The problem that confronted us now was how to take all our equipment, tool box, torches, radios, lift keys, short extension ladder etc., up six flights of concrete stairs and eventually up to the lift motor room on the roof, without disturbing the, hopefully still sleeping, suspect.

Lift rescues are attended by a pre-determined number of appliances, in this case a water tender ladder and an emergency tender (ET) which gave us a crew of seven. The ET driver stayed with his machine monitoring all radio messages both from the brigade main scheme and our short range 'hand-helds'. One man was positioned just inside the main door, partly for security reasons (he had a good view of both appliances) and partly to act as doorman for the automatically locking doors which would shut behind us every time we went outside for additional equipment.

That left the Sub and one firefighter positioned on the sixth floor landing whilst the Leading firefighter (Lf) and the other two firefighters made their way quietly to the lift motor room, using the short extension ladder to gain access via a loft type hatch. After turning off the power they radioed down to the Sub who had, by now, used the special lift key to slide back the landing door and ascertain the position of the lift car whose roof, it turned out, was just about at our floor level.

On the given order the motor room team commenced hand winding the lift car up to the sixth floor which would normally, due to the design of lifts and their counter balance weights, be the easiest option. On this occasion, however, the lads experienced some difficulty, commenting to the Lf that the car seemed unusually heavy. As the lift reached its correct position on the landing we discovered the reason for their extra effort. The doors opened, and with heads bowed and in complete silence the embarrassed plain-clothed officers left the lift car, walking briskly to the stair well door, through which they made their exit. One followed another, then another, then another, and so on. About eighth to leave was a female officer who was closely followed by a man carrying a large metal door breaker... and still they were coming. We counted twelve in all, eleven big strapping lads, one pretty young girl and the world's largest door breaker, and then, there they were... gone, leaving us to tidy up with the only word of thanks being a grunt of "Ta" from the last one to exit.

So what had happened? Our radio man had not been idle during his listening brief and had engaged the young WPC in useful conversation. It was by now approaching 7a.m. and on returning to the station we opted for an early breakfast which, to our delight, would include a full rundown of the history connected to our most recent rescue. To quote the Cornish comedian Jethro, "What 'appened was," was that apparently the Drug Squad, working on intelligence gathered over a period of time, set out to raid a flat in a particular block. They gained entry through the main door and grouped up ready for 'the bust' outside the suspect's ground floor flat. Using the door breaker, an entry was made and with lightning speed members of the team apprehended the suspect while others searched the flat for banned substances. Still half asleep and dazed by the noise and flurry of action the suspect was arrested and read his rights. "Anything you say will be............."

"Hold up," interrupted the now wakening suspect, "that's not me... I'm not 'im... he don't live 'ere." It turned out that the suspect, for whatever reason, had recently moved from his ground floor flat to one on the seventh floor. Ooops! So with a swift apology and the promise of a new front door from the council, the boys in blue, (or not, in their case) were in the lift and off to the seventh floor, a little embarrassed and even more determined to make the bust this time. And that's where the story began. How were they to know that the lift was designed with a 'max. load' of 8 persons? Oh yes, by the engraved metal panel above

the lift controls that stated, "MAX. LOAD 8 PERSONS,"... that's how. The young WPC was on patrol and driving past the flats when she heard a faint radio message asking for assistance; being inside a metal box in a reinforced concrete shaft does not help the strength of radio transmissions. She stopped her patrol car and established contact with her trapped colleagues and operation 'bungled bust' swung into operation.

The next evening it was reported in our local paper that several 'persons' were released from a lift car by Fire Service personnel at a given address. This 'limited' information was probably given to the newspaper by our control staff when reporters made their usual morning phone calls to control, enquiring as to any local incidents. The story ends there... well almost. It was over a month later when a watch member read out a story from the same local paper stating that the police categorically denied rumours that their drug squad had been rescued from a lift car in the area. But we know differently, don't we - or were we all dreaming?

MOVE AT YOUR PERIL

It is a well known fact that moving house can be one of the most stressful things a person can do. Packing up belongings you don't use or need, then unpacking them the other end so that you can not use them in the new house too. There's also the moving boxes full of items you packed for a previous move and would get round to sorting when you had some spare time. These, and all the associated trials and tribulations create short tempers and frayed nerves. Now what one doesn't need in all this, is a great lumbering dog getting under your feet. Unfortunately, Mr and Mrs Johnson had just that. They were moving themselves into a two bedroom semi one rainy and cold October morning and Otto, the old Bassett hound, was busying himself checking out the new place. Looking in this room and that room, exploring every nook and cranny of his new home, he was oblivious to how many times he was getting in the way. Poor Mrs Johnson was getting more and more stressed, and Mr Johnson was getting more and more tellings off.

Eventually, the point was reached when something had to be done, and they both agreed on the solution….. Otto. He was the main cause of the stress and therefore had to go. So even though it was still raining, he was unceremoniously turfed out of the back door and into the garden. Otto was apparently unimpressed by this decision.

Didn't these people know how important his job was? This new house had to be thoroughly checked out … it was his responsibility!

The back door was firmly closed and so Otto needed to find a new way in to allow him to complete his task.

The previous occupants had moved out the day before and had taken everything, bar the light bulbs. When they took the tumble dryer all that was left in the gap between kitchen cupboards was the 4" diameter hole which the vent pipe had been connected to. It was about 10" above the floor and obviously went through the wall to the outside. It was this hole which Otto discovered as being the only way back in to the house. Now whether he thought that he could somehow squeeze through this hole or whether he simply decided to keep an eye on these stupid humans and what they were doing in his new house, we will never know. What we do know is that his head got through, followed closely by two long droopy ears, but then no more. It was this situation which was printed on our turn-out slip as "Dog stuck in wall."

It didn't take us long to get to the house and on the way we discussed what we might be confronted with. Some months back we had rescued a Jack Russell terrier from the cavity between the inside and outside walls of a house, after he had gone in chasing a rat. We pondered the chance of this being a similar situation, but we hadn't come close to imagining what we actually were going to be confronted with. As we pulled up outside the house Mrs Johnson came running out to us in a terrible state. Mascara-stained cheeks, red shiny nose, and panic stricken eyes…we thought some terrible tragedy must have occurred inside. Were we going to be faced with some traumatic situation which would test our character and professionalism to the limit? "Quick, he's in here… will he be alright, what will you do? Oh please, please don't hurt him, quick come on." This garbled plea for help only served to heighten the tension, and we hurried in to assess the situation and decide on the best course of action. Striding purposefully through the front door we were led through to the kitchen…..

Now, try to imagine the walls of an African hunting lodge with various animal heads mounted on the walls looking noble and proud. And then imagine the head of an old droopy bassett hound with sagging eyes and jowls mounted on a wall 10" off the ground. You will perhaps be able to understand why, with our emotions wound so far up, that laughter was the only possible release. But… we are the professional Fire Service and laughter was not what Mr and Mrs Johnson wanted to hear from us at that moment so John Barker, the officer in charge, realising what was about to happen, quickly said, "Ok lads, sort it out," and guided a tearful Mrs Johnson and husband into the living room to 'take some details'.

Hysterical laughter is surprisingly hard to do quietly but we did our best. I'm sure neither Mr or Mrs Johnson was aware that we were all starting to look like her - with our tear-stained cheeks and red noses. But, after control was eventually regained, we got down to the job in hand… Saving Otto!

We tried pushing him, we tried pulling him, but Otto didn't budge. George, the cheery-faced old hand (as we call firefighters who've been in for a long time), suddenly

chirped up from outside, "You know lads, what we need is lubrication. Y'know like when you get your ring stuck on your finger and you need to soap it up to slide it off!" Now when an old hand proffers advice like this, it is a fool who dismisses it out of hand. So it was, that lubrication with soap became our plan number one. A bar of hand soap was quickly found and it fell to me to lather up the neck of this, by now, forlorn-looking creature. Unfortunately, the mixture of a greasy coat and a rather cheap bar of soap saw not a single soap sud created. So plan number two was needed… after a quick search through a box labelled 'Kitchen', a bottle of Fairy washing-up liquid was discovered and handed to me. It seems that the adverts are right after all, because with a liberal application of the liquid and a little water, I created a huge amount of white foam. Otto was singularly unimpressed with this new look but was in no position to complain. Once thoroughly lubricated we positioned ourselves fore and aft, and after a count of three, pushed and pulled together. Not unlike a bar of soap shooting out of wet hands, Otto was shot out of his hole. It now seemed that what was going on in his new house was no longer important, and without even a backward glance, off he plodded up to the top of the garden where he sat looking at us with digust.

The sight of an elderly, droolly bassett hound, trying to look aloof whilst wearing a soap sud ruff started off the hysterics again, just as John was returning to the kitchen. With a rather loud "tut" he turned on his heel and quickly bundled Mr and Mrs Johnson back into the front room to 'clarify a couple of things'.

PLEASE SIR .... do we rescue cats from trees?

"No, we do **not** rescue cats from trees. Have any of you ever seen a dead cat in a tree?" The instructor glared at the assembled recruits daring any one of them to speak. There was complete silence! He stood at the edge of his podium looking down at his highly-polished, fire service issue, Doctor Marten shoes. His left hand was thrust deep in his trouser pocket, whilst the other was resting on the end of a twelve inch wooden ruler perched on his desk. "No," he said loudly, after enjoying the moment of hush. He looked up at his captive audience, "No we haven't have we?" We knew the answer he required and without even considering the question mumbled as one voice, "No Sir."

Three years later as I stared blankly at the buildings flashing past, my memories of Training School were rekindled. I was aware that we were soon to reach our destination and thoughts of what would confront us became my priority. Would it be a fluffy kitten ten feet up a conifer crying for its mother, or some vicious hissing ball of fur with flashing green eyes and the claws of a tiger, defying anyone to remove it from its chosen vantage point. Well it was neither. In fact it was just an ordinary pussy cat whose distraught owner, a lady in her late fifties/early sixties who seemed to live only to pamper little Tiddles (all names have been changed to protect the innocent!), was in floods of tears at the foot of what must have been one of the tallest trees in Telford.

So why were the Fire Service there you may ask. Good question. I'll explain. The Instructor from The Lancashire County Fire Service Training School at Chorley was, of course, quite correct. The Fire Service do not, under normal circumstances, rescue cats from trees and if you ask them to they will, with all sympathy, and in the nicest possible way, suggest that you call the RSPCA. The RSPCA will then send one of their highly trained Officers who will assess the situation. Being a professional, he will also know that cats don't get stuck in trees, but he can tell if the animal is in a distressed state or not. If not, he will suggest that the owner (closely watched from above by the pampered puss in question) lays out some favourite tit-bits and awaits the imminent descent. On the other hand he may decide that Ginger has been scared out of his mind by some local canine thug and nothing short of a twelve bore is going to get him back on terra-firma. If the frightened feline is within reach of any ordinary ladder, and the job doesn't appear too hazardous to take on single handed, the RSPCA Officer may well tackle it alone. But in other circumstances........ well, there's no alternative - call out the Fire Service.

The longest ladder we carry on our fire engine is 45 feet (13.5m for metric readers). The tree? Well the tree was about twice that height. And Tiddles, fortunately or probably unfortunately for him, was perched at about 40 feet. Now, anyone who has ever watched the lads at work on the Station drill ground will, in most cases, be impressed by the way they throw those heavy ladders around, banging them accurately into position at the drill tower window, then scuttling up like a rat in a drainpipe to fight another imaginary fire. Easy, on flat tarmac. Easy, to a rectangular

window frame in a flat brick wall on the drill ground that you use every day. Incredibly awkward on soft, sloping ground to a 100 foot knobbly tree with branches askew and some distraught woman wailing down your right ear. But in true Fire Service spirit we set about the task in hand and although, for some of us, this was the first time we'd used a '13.5' in anger, the pitch looked good and everything was going........well, almost like clockwork. All that remained was to extend the ladder, zip up, grab Tiddles, modestly accept the thanks of the grateful taxpayer, and then it would be back to the Station for tea and sticky buns and to await the arrival of our RSPCA Commendation. Hurrah!

Oh no, not quite. You see a 13.5 metre ladder comes in three sections which are extended by way of an extending line (rope, if you're not in the Fire Service). When the order 'Extend the ladder' is given, one man steadies the handling poles, which look like two legs coming from the back of the ladder. One man 'foots the heel', that is, he stands on the bottom of the ladder to make sure it doesn't move, and the other two men pull like billi-o on the extending line. If all's going to plan, at this stage the ladder should start to extend, which it did, steadily making its way skyward towards the waiting Tiddles. As the head approached its target, the top 'rounds' or rungs started to foul on the branches and bend them upwards until the round passed and they sprung back to their original position. Oh Tiddles, why did you pick that branch to perch on? With the final heave on the line there was a 'TWANG' and then a noise like.............well, sort of like a cat screaming as it is catapulted from a tree and starts to plunge earthward from 40 feet. That noise was followed by a dull thud and yes, Tiddles was down, but surprisingly not out and after a couple of seconds of gathering his thoughts and reckoning up how many of his nine lives remained intact, he was off like a greyhound never to be seen again - at least not by us!

New recruits beware. In a situation like this it is fatal to look one's colleagues in the eye for fear that something quite unacceptable, like a smile, might issue forth, and smiles lead to giggles and so on, and so it was. Four firemen re-stowing a large, heavy ladder on the roof of a fire engine whilst desperately trying to stifle their almost uncontrollable laughter and being scowled at by their very embarrassed Sub Officer, who had been left with the unenviable task of collecting the details of the incident from the now hysterical cat owner. After much reassurance from the Sub and the RSPCA Officer about how cats always land on their feet and how a 40 foot fall is nothing to a cat and, "Oh yeh, I've seen 'em jump from twice that height on to concrete and survive," and so on, we left the scene and travelled back to the Station in near silence. The only sounds were the occasional involuntary whine or splutter of laughter from the back seat as we nudged each other and reminded ourselves of what had just occurred, knowing we were in for a roasting but making the most of these final moments of mirth like naughty boys returning disgraced from a school trip.

We accepted our roasting but argued that we really hadn't done anything wrong as far as procedures went; after all our ladder pitch was good and had Tiddles only held on a little tighter we would have been the heroes of the day.

As for the laughter, it wasn't meant to be cruel or malicious, but as I'm sure you know once you start it's very hard to stop and doubly so when you know the situation won't allow it. I still think of poor Tiddles plummeting earthwards, all four limbs stretched out horizontally, using his instinct to increase his surface area in a vain attempt to slow his descent. Nice try Tiddles. Oh, in case you're wondering, no, we never did receive our commendation, it must have got lost in the post!

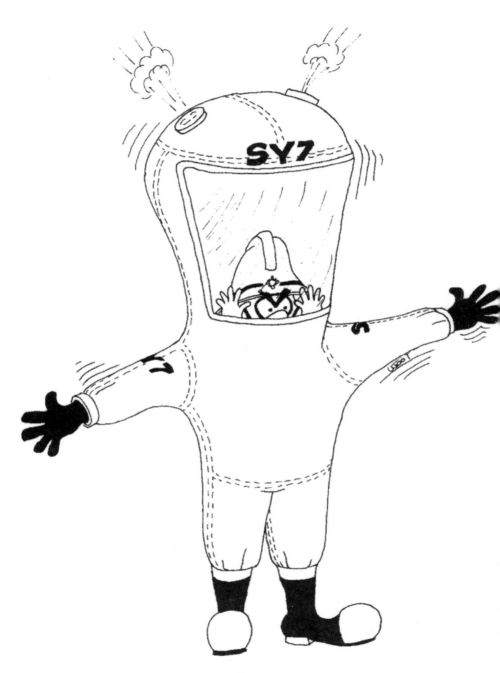

YOU'LL SEE BETTER IF YOU DON'T BREATHE

Apparently, there are over a million different chemicals that can be transported around Britain at any one time, and if any of these chemical-carrying vehicles is involved in an accident, guess who is expected to go and clear up the mess. You've got it.... The Fire Service. Now chemicals can be pretty nasty things and the last thing you want to do is risk getting them on your skin or breathe them in, so thankfully the fire service is issued with a special piece of equipment... the Chemical Protection Suit. To make sure that nothing can contaminate the firefighters, this suit totally encompasses everything - you, your fire kit, and your breathing apparatus. This means it has to be big, but here's the thing... when some civil servant was tasked with deciding about sizing these suits he had two options: one was to go for small, medium, large, and extra large, bearing in mind the different sizes of the firefighters liable to wear them. The other option was to find out the size of the biggest firefighter in Britain and make it that size. This obviously would save his department vast amounts of money and thus perhaps get him that promotion he had been looking for. So, after much measuring and complicated mathematical equations, the size was settled upon. The biggest firefighter working today was concluded to be 8' tall and weigh at least 40 stones.... because these suits are huge!

When we had our first one delivered, we were obliged to familiarize ourselves with how to get into it and all the associated technical bumph which always accompanies any new piece of equipment. I, being the tallest member of the watch, was nominated to be the guinea pig. So I put on a breathing apparatus set, my fire tunic, a hard hat, and after getting myself a hand held radio, was unceremoniously bundled into the enormous green plastic suit, forcing my hands through hard wrist cuffs so as to be able to get them into the gloves. Once inside I peered out of the large plastic window in the front and waited for suggestions as to what to do next. You can imagine, I didn't have to wait long... but I was after serious suggestions.

Now, you know what happens when you breathe on a window - it steams up, so when I breathed out my 'window' did the same, thus making it harder and harder to see out. Noting this to the rest of the gathered watch coaxed one of them to look at the instructions. "Oh," said Paul Peterson, a rather laid back, easy going firefighter, "there's a de-mister cloth in this box apparently and it says you should have it in there with you. Look at the bottom of the window, there should be a pocket for it to go in." Sure enough there was a tiny pocket and Paul helpfully opened my zip and passed a tiny cloth about 4" square to me, my de-mister! This was the point at which the biggest problem with these suits was revealed to us all. For me to do any thing within the suit, such as wiping my misted up window, I had to force my hand back through the hard cuff and take my arm fully out of my sleeve. Once within the body of the suit I could easily wipe the window and pop the cloth back into its dedicated pocket. I then had to force my hand back down the sleeve and into the glove. The thing is, as soon as I breathed out again, the same thing happened. So after a few repeats of the same drill it seemed sensible to leave my arm out of the sleeve permanently, and be ready at all times to wipe clear a little area so as to see out.

Now, the air in a breathing apparatus set is stored under pressure in a cylinder on your back. Normally when you breathe in, the air comes from the cylinder and into your lungs. When you breathe out, the air simply goes out of your mask and joins the rest of the air making up this world's atmosphere. When you are in a chemical incident suit however, the air has nowhere to go... except to start inflating the suit. This it does at an alarming rate, and the sleeve without an arm in it starts to rise higher and higher with every breath. You end up looking like some huge green alien with one arm moving wildly on its own, a misted up window at the front, and, on a cold winter's day, two jets of steam coming from the blow off valves on top of your head.

A hand-held radio is also essential because you can hear hardly anything once inside one of these suits, and if you want to have a conversation with someone, both of you need radios, even if you're standing next to each other.

So here we have it. Equipment designed to protect us from all manner of nasty chemicals, which it does very effectively. The problem is, we are expected to actually do something once encased in the suit, and that's where the job becomes a little tough. The fact that this is a gas-tight suit means nothing can get in, but also nothing, like body heat, can get out. So after quarter of an hour it starts to get a little hot, which causes you to breathe quicker, and use up your air sooner, so after twenty minutes or so, an hour and a half's worth of air is almost used up. If the incident is a long one you can imagine that there ends up being a relay set up of firefighters getting into and out of these big green suits.

One day, a few years ago in the middle of winter, we were called to a chemical spillage in a local residential street. After turning out from the fire station two chaps in the back, Dave Wilkins and Steve Podmore ,were told to put their chemical incident suits on. Now you can imagine how hard that was going to be, trying to get into an enormous green plastic suit wearing breathing apparatus, whilst being thrown around in the back of a speeding fire engine. There were arms going into leg holes, legs going into de-mister cloth pockets and all the time the destination getting closer and closer. Eventually there were two exhausted and very sweaty firefighters "rigged" and ready for action. There are a set number of appliances which are sent to different incidents; what we call the pre-determined attendance. The PDA to this job was two fire engines, a fire officer, an ambulance, and a police car. We all turned up at pretty much the same time, and proceeded to drive slowly down the street waiting for some helpful resident to come out and tell us exactly where the spillage was. No one did, but a few lace curtains started twitching as our convoy of vehicles with blue flashing lights drove past. We had to turn round at the bottom and try again as we still hadn't come

across anything even remotely suspicious. After reaching the other end again with our only success being getting more curtains twitching, it was deemed sensible to get out and walk. Three officers in charge did just that, and after walking a hundred yards or so, came across a suspicious pile of white powder. They could of course have stuck their finger in it and licked it, pronouncing clearly for all to hear, "Yes lads, it's definitely arsenic....." but that's not a particularly good idea so they called back for Dave and Steve to come and investigate. All this time these two chaps had, of course, been breathing. So now their suits were fully inflated and their screens almost completely obscured by mist. They heaved themselves out of their seats and started to walk towards the incident. You can imagine that now the lace curtains were being almost wrenched from their wires by householders aghast at what they were seeing making their way down their street. "You're not going to believe this Mable, green blinkin aliens, come and look!!!" These "aliens" eventually arrived at the pile of powder and began to investigate. It wasn't long before they looked behind the garden hedge and discovered a white plastic container. It had writing on it but their screens were so misted up they couldn't read what it said, so they showed it to the officers standing a little way back.. "What's this say?" asked Dave. "Toxic!" came the reply. "But it's spelt with a C and a K, and I think it's written in crayon!" On closer inspection words could be made out through the label with 'Tocksic' written on it. They were.... "self-raising flour." It turned out that some idiot kids had thought it would be good sport to get the fire service out to their chemical spillage and had been watching from what they assumed was a safe distance. What they didn't realise was that they had been seen pouring out the flour and their names were immediately given to the police. So, they ended up in trouble, Steve and Dave used what was left of their energy trying to escape from their alien suits and the rest of us ended the job drinking tea kindly offered by a neighbour. The end of yet another 'Day at the Office'.

CRASH BANG WALLOP

In the modern Fire Service of today you have two distinct groups. Firstly you have the 'wholetime' firefighters who work a shift system, so are only on duty when they are at work. Then you have the 'retained' firefighters. These, some would suggest, have *real* jobs and carry an alerter which lets them know when they are needed to go to an incident. At this point they race to their fire station and respond to whatever emergency they are needed at.

Since they are expected to know what they are doing in the same way as wholetime firefighters are, they need continual training to keep them familiarised with how all their equipment not only works, but can be adapted. So, every week, they get together of an evening and do "drills."

One particular week at a retained fire station near to Shrewsbury, the whole crew were at the back of the station with a 'combined drill' in full swing. There were hoses criss-crossing the drill yard, ladders of various lengths leaning against the tower, floodlights causing the reflective strips on their tunics to shine brightly, water shooting out of branches in all directions, pumps roaring, generators whining, men shouting orders at each other, and generally a quite wonderful example of organised chaos for any passerby to behold.

Once the drill had been taken as far as it could, the order "Knock off" was barked by Station Officer Clark and all the various parts of the drill were stopped and the equipment stowed once more back onto the fire engine. When everything was finished and put away it was time for the debrief .All the firemen lined up to hear Richard Clark's observations of what they had just done. He was a very smart man whose portly frame fitted rather too snugly into his freshly pressed uniform. He spoke with crisp confident tone to which everyone was compelled to listen."Well done chaps, it was good to see such enthu…" He didn't manage to finish. He was stopped by a screech of brakes, a dull thud, and a pained shout. Immediately all the gathered firefighters hot - footed it to the front of the station to see what had happened. There before them across the main road was a stationary car with the driver's door wide open but the driver still inside slumped over the steering wheel. Lying on the ground between the front and rear wheels was a body. People were already gathering to stare in morbid fascination at the scene, frozen into inactivity by the prospect of having to actually do something.

Richard Clark arrived and immediately ordered one firefighter to phone for an ambulance, one to fetch the first aid kit and the rest to follow him. It must have been a quite spectacular sight to see eighteen fully kitted up firefighters running across the road to rescue some poor unfortunate soul who'd just been run over by a car. When they arrived the Station Officer took command. One firefighter was told to check on the driver. This he did only to find she was completely unhurt but had only got as far as opening the car door before she had collapsed in a flood of tears imagining what an horrific sight she would be faced with. Richard had knelt down next to the casualty to assess his injuries. It was only then that the movements initially thought to be involuntary trauma-induced twitching were, in fact, the elderly gentleman laughing to himself. Now shock takes many forms and it is well known that people are capable of surprising reactions when suffering traumatic injuries; like the case of a man picking up his own severed arm and carrying it two miles to get help. But to laugh, when it is plain that a car has just driven over one of your legs, was quite unexpected.

There really was only one question that Station Officer Clark could ask… "Why are you laughing?"

It was only then that the elderly gentleman stopped chuckling, sat up, looked at Richard, lifted his leg from under the car and knocked on it in just the way you would knock on a door. The hollow sound made him laugh again, "Look here, hollow, it's false y' see. I'm laughing 'cos I'm glad it weren't the other one… I haven't got a spare one of them!"

YOU DON'T WANT TO PUT THAT IN THERE.....

The weather was hot and sunny; a perfect day for doing very little, a terrible day for trying to put on thick quilted fire kit in the back of a speeding fire engine. But here we were, turning out of the fire station on our fourth call out that day. "What we got?" came a shout from Jeff Pritchard, our new recruit (or "Jockey" as they are more commonly known). "Woman trapped in a fence," came the reply. Now this is often all the detail we have while we're on our way, and it is upon this that we must base our preparations. Different situations require different equipment and procedures so we have to imagine what we might possibly be faced with. Will it be someone's head stuck in railings, or perhaps a person stuck in barbed wire or, worse still, someone impaled on a spiked fence? We were left to ponder this until we eventually arrived.

We pulled up in front of the incident. We knew where it was by the number of people crowding round the unfortunate victim. There was a six foot 'larch lap' fence running from the public footpath at the front of the house right through into the garden behind. Four of us got off the fire engine leaving just the driver behind. We strode confidently up the drive to take a look at the problem.

This is the pressure moment of a job…. Everyone there is expecting us to save the day and sort out the problem with speed and efficiency. One glance and we will know exactly what to do. Now of course it is our job to deliver on those expectations regardless of what we are actually faced with. So the act begins. We use experience, common sense, training, and educated guesswork in varying proportions to convince our wage-paying public that we are worth the money and it really was a good idea to call us out.

As we approached the crowd, everyone moved away… except one embarrassed looking young lady. There she stood with her finger poking through a hole in the fence. The hole had at one time had a knot in it but, as with many fences, it had dropped out some time ago. Now it's a funny thing, but there seems to be a flaw in the human character that makes you feel compelled to stick your finger into places which common sense would suggest that you don't. This was such an occasion, but when she had pushed her finger into the hole she encountered a nail which was sticking out at such an angle that when she sharply pulled her finger out, the nail stuck into her finger and acted like a barb, rendering her well and truly 'trapped'.

She was so embarrassed and kept repeating the word "sorry" like some sort of mantra. I'm sure the fact that she was so good-looking wasn't an influence on our professionalism but there was an awful lot of uncharacteristic sympathy being offered by firefighters vying with each other to offer a kind word.

Fortunately Harry Brockhurst, our officer in charge, was concentrating on the job in hand and it was he who realised that we couldn't get to the nail to cut it away and he felt sure she wouldn't want us to cut off her finger, so we had a problem. There is a saying in the service that before you start on a plan, give the problem a "couple of coats of looking at." This, after everyone was brought back on board, was what we did. It took a minute or so during which time Jennifer (as one of the guys had instantly found out was her name) started looking more and more anxious.

Confidence returned to her face when we all, as one, 'sprang' into action. Two of us fetched our short ladder and various other pieces of equipment which could be used to brace the fence. The other firefighter fetched the electric saw and fitted the timber cutting blade with enviable prowess. Thus kitted out we braced the fence so as to make it solid. Then using the saw we cut a 12" square around her finger, so removing her from the big 6'x 6' panel. She was then able to walk to the ambulance carrying her small portion of fence and be taken to hospital where doctors with infinitely more ability could remove the nail.

Strictly speaking, the lovely Jennifer hadn't had her finger freed from being trapped but as she was able to walk away from the line of fence, we counted it as a successful rescue. I never did find out whether one of the other guys had managed to casually pop by to check how her injured finger was, but I'd put money on at least one of them doing so!

INSIDE OUT

"RESCUE PUMP TO RTC, PERSONS TRAPPED, ST GEORGE'S STREET," barked the tannoy. All the men on duty that evening rushed from where they were working to the appliance room. Those assigned to the Rescue Pump jumped aboard and started getting their fire kit on. "Where abouts on St George's Street we off to?" came a voice from the rear cab.

"Blinkin' 'eck," came the reply. "It's just round the corner, about four hundred yards up the road." Now this situation causes us a dilemma. We, as an emergency service, are expected to turn out of the station with lights flashing, horns blaring (if needed), and with as much speed as is safe; but we are also expected to be ready, when we arrive at the job, to jump out, fully kitted-up, to deal with whatever we are faced with without delay. On our way to an RTC we have a few extra things to think about, like putting on high visibility jackets, cramming our hands into surgical gloves followed by leather gloves, then locating and putting on eye protection. All of which takes time, which for this call out, we didn't have. So our quick-thinking officer in charge, Matthew Rand, shouted at the driver, "Turn your blues off and 'ang on till we're ready, no good turning up 'arf dressed!" The blues were duly turned off and the frustrated driver 'champed at the bit' for a full thirty seconds (which

of course felt like an eternity) until we were ready enough for him to turn out. Another thirty seconds later we arrived at the car crash and, like everyone expects, we jumped out ready for action.

The thing about RTCs is that we only get called to the bad ones. If the ambulance crew can get the injured people out then they will, and for the majority of incidents that's what happens. But, when it has been a nastier accident, and the people inside the vehicle are trapped, then we are called, along with some quite fantastic cutting and lifting equipment. We then free the casualties so they can be treated at the scene or taken to hospital as quickly as possible. This means that we are often faced with some pretty gruesome sights, and with the amount of blood which can be found on and around the victim, it's sometimes hard to make out exactly what it is you're looking at, and trying to deal with.

This was what we were faced with four hundred yards up the road from the fire station. A car had collided with a tree after swerving to avoid a dog. There appeared to be a huge amount of blood on and around the man and woman in the front two seats. You have to bear in mind though that if for instance, you were to spread a pint of milk around in a car, you could cover virtually all the surfaces and still have enough to create various puddles of the stuff. So, as you have a good eight pints of blood in your body, losing one pint isn't necessarily that worrying.

Anyway, the man who had been driving was in a pretty poor state and the main concentration of work began around him. His injuries were obvious and life threatening

so he had to be got out double quick. Fortunately he was to make a full recovery thanks to some sterling work of the men working on him. The lady in the passenger seat however looked comparatively unscathed and was slumped forward, being held upright by her seat belt. As soon as we arrived, it was someone's job to check on her.

Jeff Boulton was a member of the crew on that particular day and, as we were to find out later, this was his first experience of a really serious car accident. At the sight before him he simply looked stunned and stood himself back a little so as not to get in the way of those firefighters who were actually starting to do something. Matthew Rand was quick to notice Jeff's predicament and as a way of getting him occupied and away from the sight of the driver, he sent him around to the passenger side to assess the condition of the lady. This would normally have been done by the ambulance crew but they arrived at the same time as us on that day and hadn't yet had a chance to get across to her, leaving one of us, young Jeff, with the responsibility of finding out her condition.

With a grateful nod at Matthew, he quickly moved round to the other side of the car, tried the door and found it could be opened, so slowly and carefully he opened the door and leant in. He found that she wasn't trapped but because she was slumped forward her breathing was wheezy and laboured, so in an attempt to rectify this problem, he gently moved her backwards to help her to breathe more easily. It was then that he stopped, frozen for what seemed like ages, staring down to the lady's lap. There, in a horrible

bloody mass, were her insides. The seat belt must have cut her open across her abdomen and now what should have been inside, was outside. After gathering himself together, Jeff allowed her to slump forward again, just in case being upright was making the situation worse. Then, in a dazed state, he went to find Rob Milson, an old hand who never seemed fazed by anything. "Rob, can you give me a hand," was Jeff's overly casual request.

He took him to the passenger door and simply pointed towards the lady's lap and said in a trembling voice, "I don't know what to do Rob, she's cut open and her intestines are all over her lap." Rob gently moved her back to look for himself and after seeing the bloody mess, he carried on moving her into a more comfortable position and stood up. Jeff could hardly breathe in anticipation of Rob's next sentence, but it turned out not to be what he was expecting....

"You silly bugger," smirked Rob, "the only thing she's cut is her forehead; that's not her insides on her lap - she's just bled into her bag of chips!"

THE BURNT OFFERING

Christmas Day... a day for spending time with family or friends. A day to be home with the children, opening presents and having fun, or perhaps eating too much Christmas dinner and falling asleep in front of the Queen's speech. Or... for this particular year, for our particular watch, starting work at nine o'clock and staying on duty till six. It doesn't happen every year thankfully, it's simply down to how the shift rotas turn out, but this year it was us, so at nine o'clock sharp we were brought to attention on parade, ready to have the day's work detailed to us. In front of us stood Bob Grant, our Sub officer, a tall willowy man wearing trousers that were just that little bit too short. "Merry Christmas chaps. Good news for you all - as we're up to date with all our work, I think we'll have ourselves a stand down today." This meant that after doing all the routine checks of our equipment, we could please ourselves what we did for the rest of the day, as long as we didn't leave the station. A spontaneous cheer echoed around the appliance room and, after being dismissed, the quickest checks ever done were completed and off upstairs we went for a Christmas cup of tea.

Traditionally, the officers on the watch cook the Christmas dinner, with all the trimmings. I've never quite understood the sense of this. They don't cook any meal for the watch all year, and then when it comes to the most important, and some may say most complicated, they are thrust into the limelight and ' woe betide them' if they make a mess of it. So with an ongoing barrage of helpful hints from the rest of the men they set to work.

The station had been decorated with all manner of gawdy Christmas decorations to help along the Christmas spirit, but it seemed that whoever had done it had hung tinsel and baubles on anything and everything that wasn't moving at the time. So it was, that surrounded by silver tinsel and fake snow, the rest of us enjoyed our 'stand down'. Darts and snooker competitions were sorted out amid peals of laughter, which just rubbed salt into the wounds of the officers sweating it out in the kitchen.

Our morning of fun and games stayed undisturbed until twelve o'clock midday. A yell of despair from John James at missing the bullseye, was interrupted by the tannoy. "Both appliances to house fire persons reported, Jane Booth Lane." This message is just one of a few things which happen when someone dials 999 to report a house fire when someone is thought to be still inside the burning building. A police car is mobilised, as is an ambulance. Three fire engines are sent, along with a fire officer in the Incident Support vehicle. So there we were, sliding down the pole, running to the fire engines, making up just part of a collection of 'professionals' responding to an incident where someone's life was possibly hanging in the balance. It's all adrenaline-pumping stuff, and the organised chaos going on upstairs in the kitchen was happily left behind by

Bob and the other junior officer as they put on their fire kit and clambered into the passenger seats of our two fire engines.

After a five minute drive, during which time two fire-fighters on each fire engine put on breathing apparatus, we arrived at the address. We were joined almost immediately by the other services' vehicles which created an impressive collection of flashing blue lights lined up outside the house. There was smoke coming out of a downstairs window when we arrived, but, rather oddly, no neighbours at the front waving frantically as they often do.

The four men in breathing apparatus quickly jumped out of the fire engines, grabbed the hose and pulled it towards the front door. The pump started screaming as it was revved up to pump the water, and all manner of shouts rang out injecting urgency into the first attack.

All this activity happened almost instantly when we arrived because smoke was actually there for all to see, coming out of the front downstairs window. What we didn't immediately notice, due to all the commotion, was the front door being violently swung open by an angry red-faced woman. Her hair was all over the place, her clothes hidden by a grease stained apron and her arms, with rolled up sleeves, were planted firmly on her hips; a sight to put fear into the bravest of men. Standing in the doorway was obviously not sufficient to get our attention so out she came, fuming, and shouted at the top of her voice, "Oi, what the #*/#* 's going on?" Everyone stopped abruptly in their tracks. Bob and the other fire officer stepped forward to take control of the situation and perhaps calm this 'wild cat' who had just appeared out of our burning building.

"What's on fire, is there anyone else in there?" was Bob's opening question.

To which came the answer, "I'll tell you what's on fire, the #*/#* turkey's on fire, and no there's no one else in there, yet, but there's fourteen coming in twenty minutes; so unless you've got a cooked turkey on one of your fire engines you can all just #*/#* off and let me get on with sorting it out!!"

So, panic over, we very quietly put away all the equipment we had got out, turned off the blue lights, and meekly drove away, back to our respective stations. Once safely round the corner roars of laughter broke out in both machines with Bob's look of surprise at the woman's verbal assault being the focus of the 'mickey taking'. All the way back it continued, with much merriment and mirth being enjoyed. Then to top it all off, when we got back we found that the firefighters who had been left behind had made a silk purse out of a sow's ear and a full Christmas dinner was ready to be served. So with the events of the last hour being retold and embellished over and over again, we ended up having a merry Christmas after all.

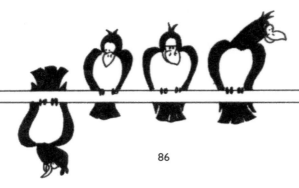

RAINING DATSUN COGS

It was one of those nights that you wouldn't even send a dog out into. Rain lashed against the fire station windows as I looked out onto the drill yard, willing the tannoy not to turn us out. My wish was granted for the next half an hour, but then at twelve o'clock midnight out boomed the unwelcome voice, "Both appliances to RTC involving HGV (we do love our abbreviations) - persons trapped." It is often the case that appalling weather as on this night can be the cause of car accidents, with the road being covered in water and the visibility being drastically cut down by rain on the windscreen. So, with the rain, wind, darkness, and cold creating challenging conditions for us to work in, we started our ten mile journey to the location of the crash.

We all take turns in the various positions on our collection of fire appliances. Number one position is the passenger seat where the officer in charge sits. Number two is the driver. Three and four wear breathing apparatus if required, and number five is the general dogsbody who has a variety of jobs depending on the nature of the call out. That night I was driving and, as it happened, was first to leave the appliance room. It truly was a horrible night and it was easy to understand how an accident could happen. The blue flashing light illuminated all the rain drops ahead and created a mesmerising scene. The talk from the guys in the back was about how we might keep the poor casualties dry and warm, because we are all aware of the 'Golden Hour'. This is the maximum amount of time we have between the accident happening and getting the injured to hospital. Any longer (depending on their injuries) can make their chances of a quick recovery less and less likely. If they are cold and wet, the odds stack against them even more. So, ready with some possible solutions, we arrived at our destination.

We were confronted by the trailer section of an articulated lorry blocking the road, and in the beams of my headlights we could see the rear end of a Nissan Bluebird. The entire roof of the Bluebird sat in a crumpled mess on top of its boot lid, and the remainder of the car was jammed underneath the trailer section.

The lorry driver, realising he had taken the wrong road had decided to turn round. He had reversed into a lane on the left hand side of the road in order to go back the way he had come. Thinking the road was clear in both directions, he had pulled out, turning right. Just as his cab had got to the left hand side of the road, the Bluebird had come round a bend a hundred yards in front of him. The car driver could see the lorry headlights on the right hand side ahead, so, as we all do at night, had kept to the left of them in order to safely pass. What he didn't realise and because of the rain, couldn't see, was that the trailer section of the lorry was still coming out of the side road, and was completely across his path. He had no time to even brake and had ploughed into the trailer at about forty miles per hour. As a result the steel beam, which runs down the length of the trailer, had sheared the roof of the Nissan off at window wiper level. Now, on my car that is about the same height as my chest, so we were preparing ourselves for at least the sight of the driver being decapitated.

Everyone knew what to do and set about doing it. I quickly got my kit on, grabbed a torch and went to investigate. The ambulance hadn't arrived yet as they had been inundated with calls because of the weather, so someone needed to assess the situation and report back to the officer in charge. That someone was me, so I crawled under the trailer to find out the number of people in the car and their condition. I shone my torch through the crumpled metalwork bracing myself for the horrific sight awaiting me.

The only person I saw to begin with was the passenger. A pair of terrified eyes blinked at me from that side of the car. It was then that I uttered those ridiculous words, considering the situation, "Are you alright?" To my utter amazement a voice came back, "Yes, I'm fine." Then I asked, "How's the driver?" and a different voice came back, "I'm fine too.." I was stunned. There were only two people in the car and both were uninjured enough to be able to answer me. Finally, and rather obviously, I said, "Don't worry, stay where you are, and we'll get you out in no time." I scrambled out from under the trailer in a daze, not quite believing what I had just found. I went straight to John Brooker, the officer in charge, and told him about the occupants of the car. His immediate reaction was one of disbelief, followed closely by suspicion I was winding him up, then delight, that this wasn't simply a body retrieval but there were live casualties in the car. The news was spread to the rest of the men and everyone set to, to get them out as quickly as possible.

The trailer was jacked up as high as it could be, a matter of about an inch, and the tyres of the car were deflated, lowering it about three inches. These two actions freed the car enough to attach a winch cable to it and simply pull it from under the trailer. As soon as it was out the woman in the passenger seat scrambled out of the now convertible car and into the shelter of the fire engine cab. When examined she was found to have no injuries at all, and explained that she had reclined her seat and was asleep when the accident had happened. While the woman was leaping out of her seat the driver was being helped out of his. He was supporting his left arm which was injured. Apparently his seat too was partially reclined and as he had hit the trailer, he had tilted his head over to one side at the very last second. The steel beam had hit his index finger knuckle, broken his shoulder, and skinned his forehead. Other than that he was completely unscathed.

If you believed in fate you would say that it wasn't their time to die that night. But I just think that I met two of the luckiest people I'm ever likely to meet…!

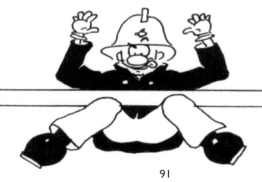

KEEP THE NOISE DOWN

There are many incidents at work which raise a smile or occasionally a roar of laughter, and although some only appear funny in the context of the day's events and do not lend themselves to paper there are many that certainly do:-

Road traffic collisions are no laughing matter as I'm sure all would agree, but as anyone whose professional life brings them into regular contact with human tragedy will confirm, a release valve is essential, and ours usually blows off (when the job is finished) with a flurry of light hearted banter. At most incidents there is something that appears hilarious after the event, such as the day when a watch from Wellington Fire Station attended an RTC on their patch and were confronted by two cars which had obviously been involved in what the BBC's Murray Walker would have called 'a coming together.' The crews of both the fire engine and emergency tender dismounted their respective appliances and with the minimum of orders from the Sub Officer set about their tasks. The early focus was on the nearest vehicle, in which persons were trapped, and as no ambulance was yet in attendance the Sub sent one man to check the other vehicle, which was some 50 metres further up the road. The firefighter he sent was an experienced hand and a much liked member of the watch whose specialism was First Aid, a skill that had earned him an instructor's certificate, enabling him to teach other members of the service. The natural choice to send? One would have thought so. After sprinting up the road he arrived at the badly-damaged vehicle that was on its roof and found that it contained one motionless casualty. After a quick check for the 'vital signs' he used another of his skills, which was to make a deafeningly loud and shrill whistle to attract the Sub's attention. All heads turned and our man, standing next to the car, made a grim face, shook his head and waved his hand, palm down, back and forth in front of his neck which we all knew meant that the casualty was a goner.

On seeing this, the 'dead' casualty let out a loud wail, probably at the thought of being pronounced dead at the scene when in fact he was suffering relatively minor injuries, and had only been knocked unconscious during the impact. It seemed that our embarrassed colleague's whistle was indeed loud enough to wake the dead. All the casualties made a full recovery (including the dead one), and in true Fire Service tradition we didn't dwell on our man's mistake... much!

A RIGHT HANDFUL

In a rural county such as Shropshire animal rescues make up a significant part of a fireman's 'on duty' life, so it was with no great excitement that the watch set off to rescue yet another entrapped horse. On arrival, a farmer, whose daughter's cherished pony had apparently leapt over a fence and wandered into a nearby slurry pit, greeted them. A rescue plan involving strops and slings was quickly put into operation and the young, newly-appointed leading fireman (Lf), eager to impress his new colleagues and more importantly the farmer's daughter, took an active roll in proceedings, getting in next to the beast to pass various ropes and slings under its belly. The atmosphere was fairly light-hearted as the crew explained to the owners that this was a 'bread and butter' type job, which rarely caused any damage to the animal, and that horse and rider would soon be reunited.

The mood, however, changed rapidly when the Lf, his hand thrust deep in the muck under the animal's gut, came out with a statement that will haunt him throughout his Fire Service career. "Oh my god," he said in a shocked and concerned tone that commanded instant attention from all present, "get a vet here quick. The poor bugger's split his stomach open, I can feel his spleen hanging out." Whilst the farmer comforted his now distraught daughter

the vet was summoned and the crews applied themselves in a more urgent fashion, fearing the worst. The poor beast was carefully pulled from the pit, the vet standing by to administer his skills to what must surely be a horrific injury.

To the surprise of all in attendance there was no blood, no gaping wound, in fact no injury at all. Could the contents of the pit somehow, miraculously, have sealed and healed such a terrible wound? Or could it be that the Lf had hold of something other than a spleen? Some other thing that you might find under the belly of a young male horse? It now became clear why the animal had stood so quietly in the pit. It wasn't that he was in agony, rather that he was quite content to be there with the nice Lf. Apparently the fire service received several letters from the horse explaining that he was stuck again and could Leading Fire-fighter Spleen (as he is now nicknamed) be sent to the rescue!